CRAYOLA
OuT-OF-THIS-WORLD
SPACE
COLORS

Laura Hamilton Waxman

Lerner Publications ◆ Minneapolis

For Bryn, Greta, Cassidy, and Signe, four girls who are out of this world

Editor's note: Many of the images included in this book have been colorized by astronomers for scientific purposes. Because these images are sourced from NASA and other scientific organizations, we believe they realistically represent the objects discussed in the text.

Lerner Publications Company
An imprint of Lerner Publishing Group, Inc.
241 First Avenue North
Minneapolis, MN 55401 USA

For reading levels and more information, look up this title at www.lernerbooks.com.

Main body text set in Mikado a.
Typeface provided by HVC Fonts.

Designer: Viet Chu

Library of Congress Cataloging-in-Publication Data

Names: Waxman, Laura Hamilton, author.
Title: Crayola out-of-this-world space colors / Laura Hamilton Waxman.
Other titles: Out-of-this-world space colors
Description: Minneapolis : Lerner Publications, [2021] | Includes bibliographical references and index. | Audience: Ages 5–9 | Audience: Grades K–1 | Summary: "From red planets to blue stars, space is full of color! Introduce young readers to the sun, moon, stars and more in this vibrant Crayola title."– Provided by publisher.
Identifiers: LCCN 2019042919 (print) | LCCN 2019042920 (ebook) | ISBN 9781541577558 (library binding) | ISBN 9781728400624 (ebook)
Subjects: LCSH: Astronomy—Juvenile literature. | Planets—Juvenile literature. | Colors—Juvenile literature.
Classification: LCC QB46 .W35 2021 (print) | LCC QB46 (ebook) | DDC 523—dc23

LC record available at https://lccn.loc.gov/2019042919
LC ebook record available at https://lccn.loc.gov/2019042920

Manufactured in the United States of America
1-46778-47769-1/30/2020

TABLE OF CONTENTS

A SKY FULL OF COLOR

What do you see when you look up at the sky? A yellow sun? White stars and a silver moon?

Deeper in space, you'll find many more colors. Let's explore some of them.

What colors can you see in this cloud of space dust and gas?

SHINING SUN AND MOON

The sun looks like a bright orange ball of fire. It's a star made of exploding gases. The sun's heat warms our planet.

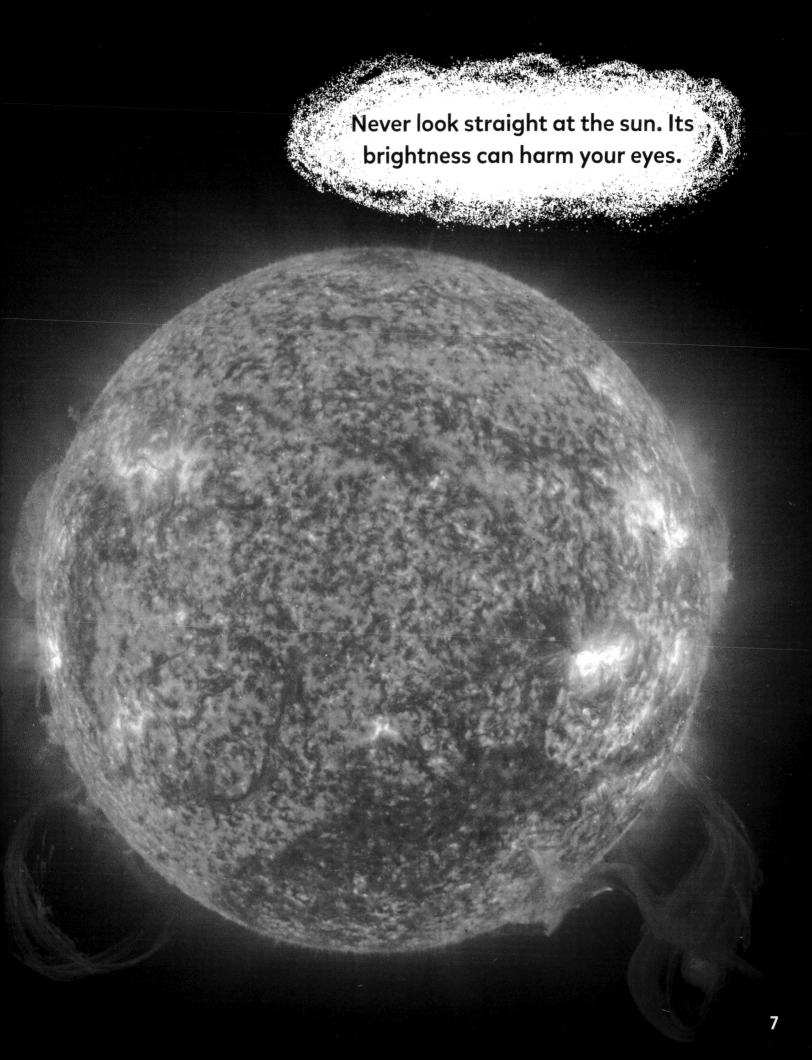

Never look straight at the sun. Its brightness can harm your eyes.

The sun shines on the moon like a lamp. It makes the moon glow white most nights.

Sometimes the moon
is low in our sky.
Then it turns orange
and red.

A RAINBOW OF PLANETS

Earth is a world of color. It has blue oceans, brown land, green forests, and white clouds.

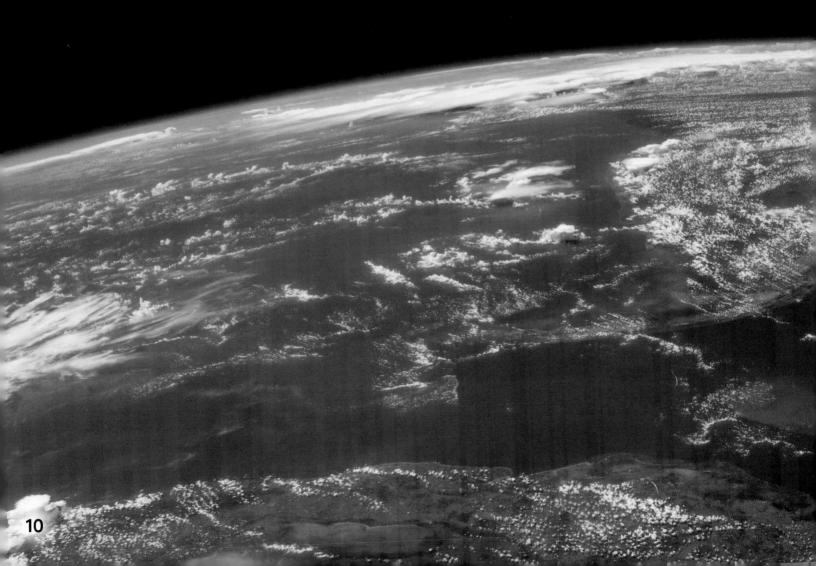

Mercury is a little
bigger than our moon.

This gray planet is Mercury.
It orbits closest to the sun.

Venus is called Earth's twin because the planets are nearly the same size.

Venus is surrounded by a thick, colorful atmosphere.

Mars is Earth's next-door neighbor in space. Astronomers have sent rovers to explore Mars's surface. The rovers take pictures and collect brick-red rocks.

Mars is known as the Red Planet.

Jupiter is the largest
planet in our solar system.

Giant Jupiter has some wild weather.
The Great Red Spot is a storm that
has lasted for hundreds of years.

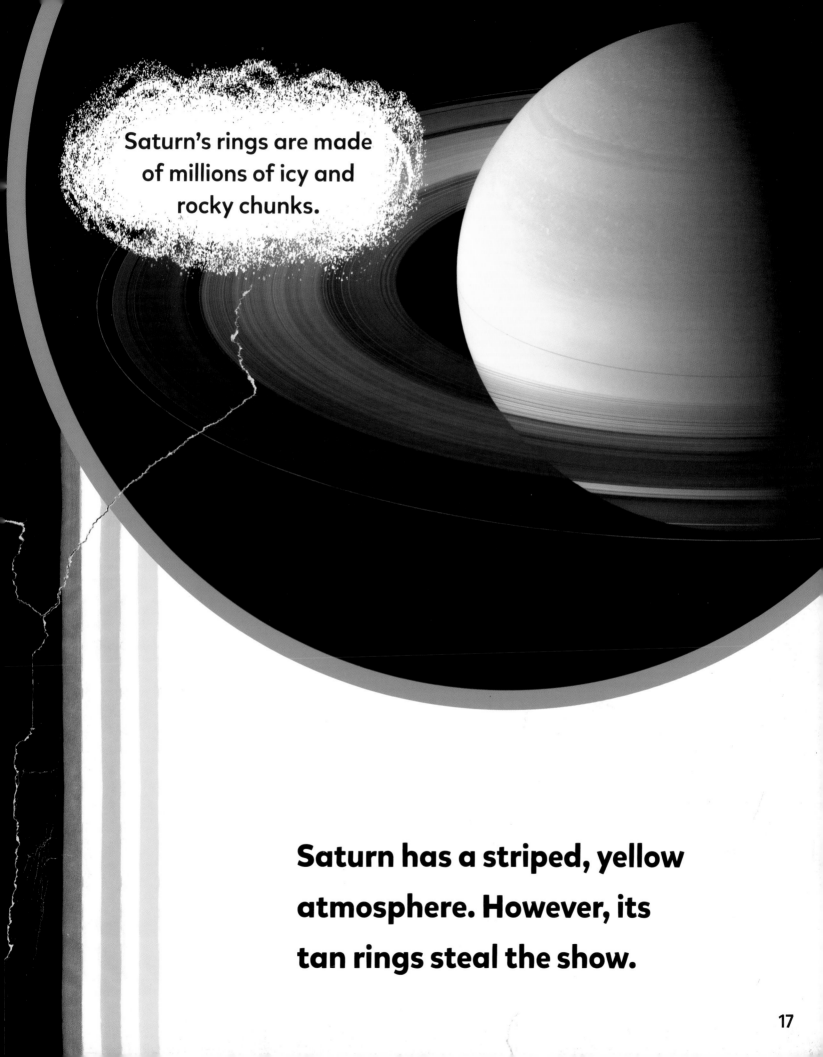

Saturn's rings are made of millions of icy and rocky chunks.

Saturn has a striped, yellow atmosphere. However, its tan rings steal the show.

Uranus is icy because it orbits far from the sun's warmth.

Uranus looks like a big, pale blue balloon. Astronomers call it an ice giant.

Blue Neptune is the windiest planet in the solar system. The winds push thin, white clouds around Neptune's atmosphere.

FAR, FAR AWAY

Stars look white in our nighttime sky . . . but look again. The hottest stars glow blue. The coolest are red. The stars in the middle shine yellow, orange, or white.

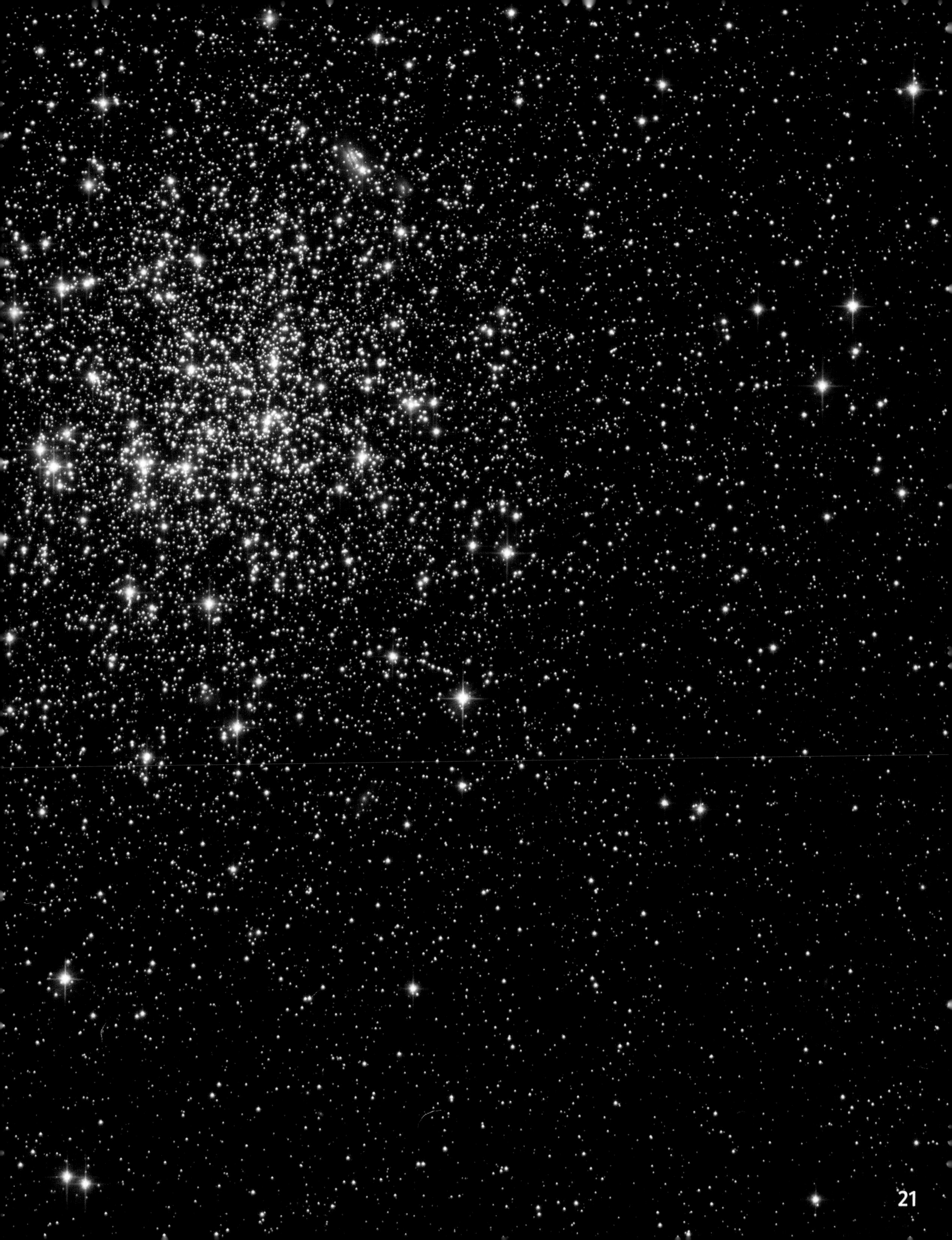

Nebulas are huge clouds of gas and dust. They look like puffs of gold, pink, red, and orange. Inside, new stars are being born.

Astronomers can take pictures of faraway nebulas using telescopes.

This swirl of brown, blue, peach, and pink is a galaxy. Galaxies have billions of planets and stars.

Space might seem like
a dark, empty place.
But it's full of colorful
planets, stars, and more!

OUR SOLAR SYSTEM

Moon

Mars

Earth

Venus

Mercury

Sun

Jupiter

Saturn

Uranus

Neptune

MANY COLORS

Space is full of color! Here are some of the Crayola® crayon colors used in this book. Can you find them in the photos? Which are your favorites?

Tickle Me Pink

Dandelion

Caribbean Green

Bittersweet

Sky Blue

Orchid

Orange

GLOSSARY

astronomers: people who study space

atmosphere: a layer of air and clouds that surrounds a planet

galaxy: a large group of stars, planets, nebulas, and dust in space

nebulas: large clouds of dust and gas in space

orbits: travels around the sun

rovers: machines that travel across a planet or moon to explore it

solar system: a group of planets that orbit a star, such as the sun

surface: the outer part of a planet or other object

TO LEARN MORE

Books

Moon, Walt K. *Let's Explore the Stars*. Minneapolis: Lerner Publications, 2018.

Pierce, Nick. *Space*. Mankato, MN: Book House, 2019.

Prokos, Anna. *Star Light, Star Bright: Exploring Our Solar System*. Egremont, MA: Red Chair, 2017.

Websites

Crayola: Spacey Shapes Coloring Page
https://www.crayola.com/free-coloring-pages/print/spacey-shapes-coloring-page/

NASA Science: Space Place
https://spaceplace.nasa.gov/kids/

National Geographic Kids: Passport to Space
https://kids.nationalgeographic.com/explore/space/passport-to-space/

INDEX

PHOTO ACKNOWLEDGMENTS

Image credits: Nick_Pandevonium/Getty Images, p. 3; va103/Getty Images, p. 4; ESO, p. 5; SOHO (ESA & NASA), p. 7; Mimi Ditchie Photography/Getty Images, p. 8; Westend61/Getty Images, p. 9; NASA, pp. 10–11, 19; NASA/Johns Hopkins University Applied Physics Laboratory/Carnegie Institution of Washington, p. 12; AXA/ISAS/DARTS/Damia Bouic, p. 13; NASA/JPL-Caltech, pp. 14, 18; NASA/JPL-Caltech/MSSS, p. 15; NASA/JPL-Caltech/SwRI/MSSS/Kevin M. Gill, p. 16; NASA/JPL-Caltech/Space Science Institute, p. 17; NASA and the Hubble Heritage Team (STScI/AURA)/P. Goudfrooij (STScI), pp. 20–21; NASA, ESA, and the Hubble Heritage Team (STScI/AURA), pp. 22–23; NASA, ESA, S. Beckwith (STScI), and the Hubble Heritage Team (STScI/AURA), pp. 24–25; Laura Westlund/Independent Picture Service, pp. 26–27; NASA/ESA/M. Robberto (STSI/ESA) and the Hubble Space Telescope Orion Treasury Project Team, pp. 28–29.

Cover and title page: Carina Nebula: Nathan Smith, University of Minnesota/NOAO/AURA/NSF; Neptune: NASA; Supernova 1987A: NASA, ESA, R. Kirshner (Harvard-Smithsonian Center for Astrophysics and Gordon and Betty Moore Foundation), and M. Mutchler and R. Avila (STScI); Venus: NASA/JPL; Cone Nebula: ESO; Jupiter: NASA/JPL-Caltech/SwRI/MSSS/Gerald Eichstadt/Sean Doran; Pillars of Creation: NASA, ESA, and the Hubble Heritage Team (STScI/AURA).